Lunar Moths
Jo Haslam

Smith/Doorstop Books

Published 2004 by
Smith/Doorstop Books
The Poetry Business
The Studio
Byram Arcade
Westgate
Huddersfield HD1 1ND

Copyright © Jo Haslam 2004
All Rights Reserved

ISBN 1-902382-68-4
Typeset at The Poetry Business
Printed by Peepal Tree, Leeds

The Poetry Business gratefully acknowledges the help of
Kirklees Metropolitan Council and Yorkshire Arts.

Acknowledgements
to *Dreamcatcher, Envoi* and *Pennine Platform* in
which some of these poems have appeared.

CONTENTS

5	Lunar Moths 1
6	Lunar Moths 2
7	Mediterranean
8	Birthright
9	Lunar Moths 3
10	Spell
11	Airborne
12	Lunar Moths 4
13	Our Neighbour
14	Borderland
16	Leggers
16	Swift in Autumn
17	Returned
18	Tulip
19	Bird Table
20	Bread
21	Tree
22	Hartstongue Fern
23	Lunar Moths 5
24	Woodbine

For Anna, Luke and Joel

LUNAR MOTHS I

You were trapping moths in a jar
and shaking them out of the open window.
Each time you put one out, another
flew in – the last completely black
with silky pleated wings. The moths
this summer are all shapes and sizes –
we examine one that's flat against the wall,
not sure if it's real. It's some tertiary colour,
a mix of silver, pink and cream
that merges with our unpainted plaster.
You reach towards it carefully as I start
to tell you about moths on polar ice caps.
You don't want to believe this,
think moths belong with evenings
when the colours are intense, the nights
deep blue; we're driving home,
moths are shooting past the windscreen.
And true, they mostly fly in summer
and all of them will come after dark,
to any light – *Ermine, Lunar Thorn*,
noctuids, loopers, the black one you set free
is *Chimney Sweeper*, and those that swing
before us on the road and punctuate the night,
round here they call them *Ghosts;*
the way they flicker suddenly and seem to die,
and those likewise, very still inside the lampshade
that, just before we sleep, stutter into life.

LUNAR MOTHS 2

No-one else but us, driving through the midnight,
hedges thick with foxglove, fern and white moon daisies.
It is July. Our son is sleeping in the back,
his second year of illness.
Minutes ago he'd stood against a lighted door,
a stripe of gold had fallen on the path,
now moonlight's washing over him.
I listen for the snore that has become habitual
these past few months, but tonight he's quiet
and we're both lulled to silence, on the twisting
road for home, as the earth falls away from us
and at every loop and rise, white moths
are thrown up, snow flurries in the headlights
as if we'd summoned them out of the hollows;
when it's only that they scent each other
in the night and strong-smelling plants attract them.
I wonder if they are the same as those that gather
in the honeysuckle at our door, large white
lunar moths that rush out of the dark to any light;
though it's said they're only drawn
by the seeming greater dark behind.

MEDITERRANEAN

The best part of the week, just to look at the sea
true to the postcard's blue, until a mist rolled in.
From our hill we seemed to hover
over cloud.; the sea was sky. And when
you called the car's sun roof a moon roof –
well I said, it could be both.

But when you asked the difference
between sea and ocean, we had to look it up –
each of them our dictionary says
is *a great expanse of water* but then
it says the ox-eye daisy is *a night flowering plant
of the convolvulaceae* and moon
*is a system of printing for the blind, in large
embossed characters.* I think about the picture
someone took at night; the moon wobbling
above a sea that tilted to the right,
and I thought of that moon how it came up
large and full as we walked along the front;
how we taught the baby to say moon,
and he said it all the way home
pointing to every round street light.

BIRTHRIGHT

I'd like to think good things will come to you
but every list I make comes back to negatives ;
beauty not lost, talents not wasted,
heart not cut in two.

And I can't predict you'll keep your own teeth,
clean lungs, a full head of hair, friends
your friends forever; when all the things
you might call birthright are just gifts
that any time could disappear.

That you survived at all was down to medicine,
not luck, so why should we believe the signs ;
the fortunate third child, your hand
that promises long life. And if you prove your fortune
every time you breathe why ask for more
than enough food, cash to get by; that love
won't desert you?

As for me, enough to believe my ears, my eyes.
Just when I thought I wouldn't hear it any more
your voice on the phone; or underneath our door
the line of light that says you're home.

LUNAR MOTHS 3

That year the house was full of moths
rising from the skirting boards and flitting
suddenly from cupboards and drawers.
We didn't know the damage till we found
long trails of silver on your winter coat,
small holes in a favourite sweater.
We thought they came with the stuff
our son bought when he was ill: old books,
magazines, second hand clothes.

I looked them up, drawn by the names
Alchymist, *Uncertain*, but you said *pests*,
and shook drops of cedarwood on collars and cuffs,
slipped soaked sachets between folds;
then for weeks I picked up small mummy cases,
prised wings open, stared at the tiny faces,
felt a superstitious prickle when I found
tell-tale indentations in the pile on your best jacket,
a fine wool scarf reduced to lacework.

So I searched through and shook out
all our clothes, hoped I'd surprise the grubs
secretly burrowed in the layers of wool
but the opened wardrobe just released the smell
of cedarwood and when I stirred hems
and sleeves, shiny winged new moths rose up.

SPELL

When the man has gone from the house
the children come to my bed.
They make a close dark tent of the blankets
and we sleep late in a fug of heat and sweat,
wake to a tangle of limbs, the cat's weight
on our legs. And I go to the barn and bring back
a clutch of warm eggs; blow the embers alive
that have almost died in the grate. Then we warm our feet
and eat toast, while the light at the window changes
wind blows the grass like a wave, the cats purr
and doze, the dog grunts with content and I know
I'll remember it all to the hour and the day
when my legs seem to float, my arms
are empty and light, the fire is cold in the grate
the barn door bangs on it's hinges; when the man
is gone from the house, the hens
won't lay and the wall-eyed dog barks all night
because children and cats won't stay.

AIRBORNE

All birds have hollow bones; which helps
to keep them airborne. Think of the redshank's
swift and slanting flight over lonely saltmarsh;
the owl's wingbeats at night, geese
whose call wakes the souls of the dead; and think
how close the myth of bird to what it is,
like the swallow who brings luck to the house
it nests on. This makes me think of you
and how sometimes it seems your bones
are hollow too; – my way of saying
I understand your need to go, but can't deny
my need to have you close.
Though when I think of the weight of your bones
I can't believe how light they've been – that's gone,
but still, like Lir who ached to have his children
in his arms I dream you back – sweat on your skin,
small bubbles blown at your mouth, backbone
like string; the spokes of your elbows folded like wings.

LUNAR MOTHS 4

Even polar ice caps have their share of moths
trawling the white peaks, wings fragile as candy-floss
quivering in the freezing air – one touch
on those peaks, you'd think they'd dissolve,
rather think of summer – moths fluttering and luminous
that come into the house suddenly at dusk
and shake the lampshade with that fast whirring sound
or those that veer towards us on country roads
at night – the *ghosts* or *souls* that appear
and disappear in the headlights.

OUR NEIGHBOUR

gets up early
in the chill winter dawn,
its cold blue light.
His blonde wife still asleep
snuffles in the pillow;
his two nearly teenage daughters, similarly.
He cracks the ice
on a bowl put out for the hens last night
feels his knuckles stick
before he frees the water underneath.

He rubs the red tip of his nose
and blows into his tingling hands
then makes for the barn.
All across the yard, his boots ring.
He does the rounds, cows and black
faced sheep, hens and geese.
He checks the gates and fences.
When he next looks up
the sun's a ball of fire in the east.

BORDERLAND

We went out tonight with lamps
to look for you in the gloomy dark – late
and there are no lights on the road
on the edge here of the county and the moors,

– we have only one neighbour,
his house across the border, next to ours;
at night we hear him knock his pipe out
on the hearth and clear his throat.

Odd, the way this land's divided –
his garden runs past our front door
and in to Lancashire, while at the back
the line runs down to join our party wall;

even so our bedroom windows both look out
to where grass and sky meet;

– dusk, we watch the moon come up
pool the hill with brilliance
but cloud has covered it tonight
and you are coming home after the late shift ,
up the icy sheep track, skidding
on the frosted pebbles.

A short cut once, you chanced the river
in the tricky moonlight, jumped
and missed your footing.

You tipped your boots out on our doorstep –
freezing water, ice and mud
and when you took it off, your coat so stiff
it stood by itself.

Cold springs sometimes they find
the early lambs huddled
in the shelter of a wall,

men too, our neighbour says
floundered off course in the cold drift
of white. They'd cross from Yorkshire
to Lancashire, again and again
when if they'd known, just half a mile away
the snow was thickening around some isolated farm,

and dozing now I almost hear a plaintive bleat,
a soft desperate shoosh, of someone pushing
through a weight of snow. I half believe
it, turn towards you but you're fast asleep,
already slipped past me, out and under the border.

LEGGERS

All the while tuned to the rasp of a nail;
scrape of a boot; spurt of a match,
bump of a boat as it nudges the wall,
trickle and slip of damp from the roof.
Tensed muscle and sweat
then push like a mole through the tunnel.
For three miles accustomed to what seems
like night. Except they're not blind.
More like dumb to say how they're dazzled
each time by what grows from a pinhole of light.

SWIFT IN AUTUMN

There is gold; there is brown;
there is mazy line pattern.
I skim the zigzag field, dip
the slide of the river
downswoop to silver
– there is bright; there is shadow;
blue glass shine. I flick
flicker, downtwist the spine
of the valley. Here is cloud under
and wet gleam of rain.

RETURNED

as in the dream where you walk in
trailing leaves and mud
as if you'd come from some deep pool
or river silting up.

But after all no dream – just you
shaking your clothes free of dust
and dirt they'd gathered these past months.

Outside the horse is lying down in the field.
Frost on the grass. Trees just past russet.
No need to say a word. This is the place
to satisfy your hunger and your thirst

and you've come back –
like those birds who can't resist
the urge that sends them out across the map
then tugs them back to earth.

TULIP

You have to plant the tulips deep
in winter, in cold compost
push them down a good six inches
so your fingers feel the earthy chill
though where I live, here in the north
it's cold enough at the start of autumn –
September this year, already night frost,
a breath of white films the ground;
you wouldn't think they'd survive
what's to come, but they need it, cold
and ice, that and the push of dark
sets them off so the roots take hold .

But outside now with trowel and tub
the bulb in my hand, solid and brown
it's hard to believe, the embryo
flower at its heart will find it's way
from underground. As likely, a pebble
picked up on the beach, a speckled eggstone
rolled in the palm, when it's warm enough
might release a fabulous bird,
as the tulip bulb when the cold recedes
might send up a small green snout
then petal edge to petal edge the silky span
is shaken out , pink and red or flame streaked.

BIRD TABLE

For the many kinds of love, read bird.
Lark that sings its heart out. Phoenix
fabled for its flame. Sparrowhawk
who strikes without hesitation.
Heron transformed in flight. Goose
whose bones are used for divination.
Cuckoo, careless, innocent;
its young who learn early
betrayal and abandonment. Swan
whose song is unquenchable grief.
Kingfisher whose other name is Halcyon.
Magpie the thief. Blackbird oblivious,
singing to the darkening blue. Dove
who returns with news of the flood.

BREAD

The field of grain the wind blows through.
The bowl of flour and salt made hollow.

The risen dough which fills the bowl.
The proven dough which holds its shape.

The field of rye the water swells.
The field of wheat or corn made gold.

The good loaf baked which knocked rings true.
The good loaf cut which makes the meal.

The loaf we break, the crust and middle.
The wafer on the tongue we take.

The grain, the water and the salt
the bread we eat, the thirst we slake.

TREE

I am the rough bark and the smooth
I am the new and withered leaf
I am the sapling and the root
the bole, the crown and the green branch
the oak and larch , the birch that bends
I am the ash key in the wind.

I am the soft wood and the heart
I am the blossom white in May
the palmate and the pinnate wand
the buried seed, the winter wreath
the needle on the forest floor
the shadow on the frosted field
the pine the cedar and the beech
I am the evergreen.

HARTSTONGUE FERN

For years it flourished on the mill wall
by our house. Some blown spore had taken
and it grew, high up, clinging to a crevice
between stone. No soil to speak of
but it loves the limey mortar
Pylitis Scolopendrum – long crinkled leaves,
Primitive and lush, and yes, tongue like.

When they pulled the mill down I thought – too late
to rescue it; and though I dug the buried leaves
and exposed root ball from the rubble, it didn't thrive.

I've taken to gardening now – know better
how to nurture plants, make soil fertile
keep slugs away, when to prune and divide –
and I know how something can still root
when everything's against it.

So I keep an eye out, for it growing wild ,
ready to prise it from a wall
or bit of stony ground, roots intact;
or hope another blown spore will take –
happenstance, or the earth asserting itself
in my garden, as it will given half a chance.

LUNAR MOTHS 5

On the wing from April to August
at night, or dusk, white, grey and cinnabar

Dark Sword Grass, Clouded Buff, Rosy Footman

all these warm months as if they belong here
though most are making their way
from the south to Iceland,

Latticed Heath, Clouded Magpie, July Highflyer

on this road, between hedgerows
with the moon coming up, hills rimmed with light,
they lift and billow in front of us

Little Thorn, Round Winged Muslin

small snowy gusts. Hold out your arms
turn your face up. They might brush your skin,

Mullein, Dusky Clearwing, Mother of Pearl.

WOODBINE

Our honeysuckle's broken loose,
hangs free of the wall
sends out suckers and side shoots
rooting itself where it chooses;
lonicera, common woodbine,
no-one knows why it twines clockwise;
but cut back hard to the woody stem
its questing tips probe out again
spiral round a fence or gate; of all our plants
the most tenacious – it flowers twice
a pink and cream mass of blooms;
the bees in it loud all this June,
night flying moths, drawn by its perfume.